What's in this book

This book belongs to

_____

1 Learn about China 中国知多少

Country profile 国家概况

China is a country in Asia. Here are some facts about China.

中华人民共和国于 1949 年 10 月 1 日成立，定都北京。

Country: China, 中国 (Zhongguo)
China is officially called the People's Republic of China (PRC).

Capital: Beijing
Located in northern China, Beijing is the political and cultural centre of China.

中国幅员辽阔，有不同的地形地貌，形成风格各异的自然景观。

Size: Around 9,600,000 km²
China looks like a huge rooster on the map. There are many rivers, lakes, mountains and forests in China.

the Li River

the Himalayas

喜马拉雅山脉是世界上海拔最高的山脉。

the Yellow River

黄河是中国的第二长河，中国人称其为"母亲河"。

Population: Over 1.3 billion
China has the largest population in the world.

Ethnic groups: 56   56个民族有各自的风俗习惯，且绝大多数民族都有自己的语言。
Besides the largest ethnic group, Han, which makes up over 90% of the population, there are also 55 ethnic minorities.

Han

Mongol

Bouyei

Yi

表中的Mandarin指的是包含北京官话、东北官话等的官话方言。普通话是基于北京官话发展而来的。英语中有时会用Mandarin来指代普通话。

Language: There is only one writing system in China, but people speak different dialects.

Written	Spoken	
Official	Official	Main dialects
Standardized Chinese characters	Putonghua (Standardized form of the spoken Chinese based on Mandarin)	Mandarin, Wu, Xiang, Gan, Hakka, Min, Cantonese

Symbols of China 中国象征

Is there anything that reminds you of China? Look at some symbols of China.

问问学生他们心目中的龙的形象。告诉学生，龙在中国文化中有重要的地位。人们每逢佳节会舞龙，端午节赛龙舟，还会将龙的形象运用于建筑装饰、服饰设计等等。在古代，龙还是帝王的象征。

The Chinese dragon: It is regarded as a divine creature and a symbol of good luck and power. Chinese people call themselves Descendants of the Dragon.

"大熊猫"一般称为"熊猫"或"猫熊"。

The giant panda: It is China's national treasure and the symbol of WWF. It is listed as one of the vulnerable species in the world.

问问学生是否在动物园见过大熊猫。告诉他们，大熊猫生活在中国海拔两三千米的竹林里，靠吃竹子为生。它们爱吃吃睡睡，也爱爬树嬉戏。

Brain teaser

What is a panda's biggest wish?

(To take a colour photo.)

长城经历了前前后后两千多年的修筑，历代总长度达两万多千米，可以环绕地球赤道半圈。

The Great Wall: In ancient times, it was built for protection against invasions. Today, it is a World Heritage site.

世界遗产（World Heritage）是一项由联合国支持、联合国教育科学文化组织负责执行的国际公约建制，以保存对全人类都具普遍价值的独特文化古迹和自然景观为目的。

中国功夫有多种门派，如太极拳（T'ai chi）、咏春拳（Wing Chun）、少林功夫（Shaolin Kungfu）等等。李小龙（Bruce Lee）是著名的功夫巨星。

Chinese kungfu: It is not only about fighting and self-defense, it can also strengthen the body and mind.

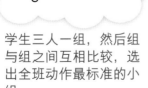

Can you do these kungfu stances?

学生三人一组，然后组与组之间互相比较，选出全班动作最标准的小组。

2 Chinese zodiac 生肖

1 Do you know the 12 zodiac animals? Learn about them.

2 niú 牛

9 hóu 猴

7 mǎ 马

3 hǔ 虎

5 lóng 龙

12 zhū 猪

The Chinese zodiac is a cycle of 12 lunar years. Each year is represented by an animal. The animals appear in a fixed order.

1 shǔ 鼠

10 jī 鸡

6 shé 蛇

4 tù 兔

11

8 yáng 羊

gǒu 狗

生肖，是中国一些民族用来代表年份的十二种动物，统称为十二生肖，即鼠、牛、虎、兔、龙、蛇、马、羊、猴、鸡、狗、猪。每个人都以其出生年的象征动物作为生肖，所以中国民间常以生肖计算年龄。

2 The 12 zodiac animals appear in the following order. Look at the pictures on page 6 again and number them.

1 rat   2 ox   3 tiger   4 rabbit

5 dragon   6 snake   7 horse   8 sheep

9 monkey   10 rooster   11 dog   12 pig

3 Which zodiac animal sign were you born under? Look at the information below to find out.

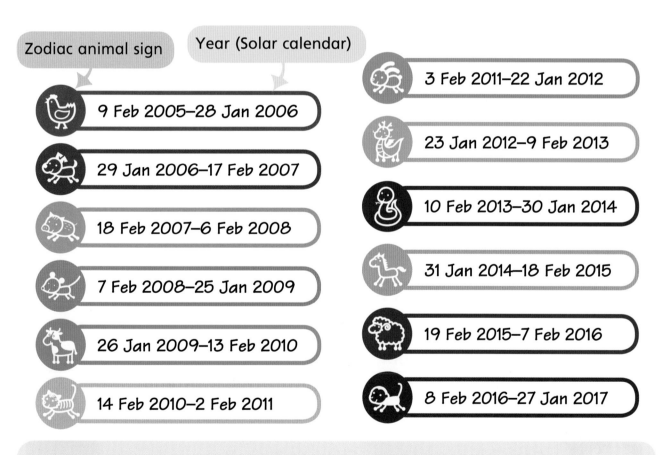

Zodiac animal sign   Year (Solar calendar)

9 Feb 2005–28 Jan 2006

29 Jan 2006–17 Feb 2007

18 Feb 2007–6 Feb 2008

7 Feb 2008–25 Jan 2009

26 Jan 2009–13 Feb 2010

14 Feb 2010–2 Feb 2011

3 Feb 2011–22 Jan 2012

23 Jan 2012–9 Feb 2013

10 Feb 2013–30 Jan 2014

31 Jan 2014–18 Feb 2015

19 Feb 2015–7 Feb 2016

8 Feb 2016–27 Jan 2017

Date of birth: _____ (Date) _____ (Month) _____ (Year)

Your animal sign: [_____] (Draw the sign)

延伸活动：让学生算算自己父母或兄弟姐妹的生肖。

3 Festivals 节日

Traditional Chinese festivals 传统中国节日

Traditional Chinese festivals are celebrated according to the Chinese Lunar Calendar. Learn the names of the most popular ones.

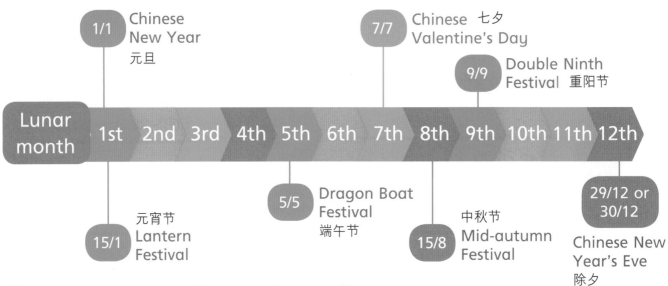

1/1 Chinese New Year 元旦

7/7 Chinese 七夕 Valentine's Day

9/9 Double Ninth Festival 重阳节

Lunar month | 1st 2nd 3rd 4th 5th 6th 7th 8th 9th 10th 11th 12th

15/1 元宵节 Lantern Festival

5/5 Dragon Boat Festival 端午节

15/8 中秋节 Mid-autumn Festival

29/12 or 30/12 Chinese New Year's Eve 除夕

Chinese New Year (Spring Festival)

1 Learn about Chinese New Year.

Chinese New Year falls on the first day of the first Chinese lunar month. This is usually in February in the Gregorian calendar.

For Chinese people, Chinese New Year is the most important festival of the year. All family members get together and there are many different customs for the festival.

中国人过春节已有4000多年的历史。在现代，人们把春节定于农历元月初一，但一般至少要到元月十五新年才算结束。

Decorations, red packets and traditional snacks represent good luck, good health and good fortune. People use unique sayings to greet each other and express good wishes.

New Year decorations

Red packets and traditional snacks

Greetings

There are various celebrations. Some people go to the temples to make wishes.

Dragon dance

Parade

Temple fair

Today, Chinese New Year is celebrated in many major cities around the world.

Beijing, China

San Francisco, USA

London, UK

2 Learn to make Chinese New Year decorations. Colour the words black or gold.

新　年　快　乐

老师可准备红纸，先用铅笔在纸上写好字，然后让学生用粗笔描写，制成新年装饰。

Dragon Boat Festival

1 Learn about the Dragon Boat Festival.

The Dragon Boat Festival falls on the fifth day of the fifth lunar month. This is usually in June in the Gregorian calendar.

During this festival, people race dragon boats and eat *zongzi*. People believe that this festival commemorates the famous poet Qu Yuan.

Dragon boats are shaped like dragons. Accompanied by rapid drum beats, the oarers pull the oars.

Zongzi are glutinous rice dumplings wrapped in reed or bamboo leaves.

2 Look at the posters of the Dragon Boat Festival. Design your own and show it to your friends.

屈原，战国时期楚国人，早年他协助楚怀王使楚国国力增强，但是后来却被楚怀王疏远。当楚国投入秦的怀抱时，屈原愤而辞官流落到汉北。流放期间，屈原创作了大量文学作品，在作品中洋溢着为民报国的热情。公元前278年，秦国攻破了郢都，屈原投江而死。传说当地百姓投下粽子喂鱼以此防止屈原遗体被鱼所食。以后每年的农历五月初五端午节，人们吃粽子，划龙舟以纪念这位伟大的爱国诗人。

Mid-Autumn Festival

1 **Learn about the Mid-Autumn Festival.**

The Mid-Autumn Festival falls on the fifteenth day of the eighth lunar month. This is usually in October for the Gregorian calendar.

This festival is celebrated at night under the autumn full moon. A popular legend goes that Chang'e, the Moon Goddess, lives on the moon.

At the Mid-Autumn Festival, family and friends get together to watch the full moon and eat mooncakes to show family unity. Children like to play with lanterns.

2 **Look at the traditional lanterns and design one for yourself. Show it to your friends.**

传说嫦娥本是后羿之妻，后羿射下九个太阳后西王母赐其不老仙药，但后羿不舍得吃下，就交于嫦娥保管。当后羿门徒蓬蒙逼迫嫦娥交出仙药时，嫦娥无奈情急之下吞下仙药，便向天上飞去。当日正是八月十五，月亮又大又亮，因不舍后羿，嫦娥就停在了离地球最近的月亮，从此长居广寒宫。后羿回家后心痛不止，于是每年八月十五便摆下宴席对着月亮与嫦娥团聚。

4 Food and drink 饮食

Chinese cuisine 中国菜

1 Chinese cuisine is an important part of Chinese culture. Learn about it.

中国菜的特点为：色、香、味、意、形、养，被称为"食材六品"。

Chinese cuisine emphasizes colour, flavour and taste.

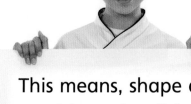

This means, shape and nutrition of a dish are also important.

2 Chinese cuisines vary in styles. The 'Eight Cuisines' of China are from these provinces.

Eight Cuisines of China

1 Anhui cuisine
2 Guangdong cuisine
3 Hunan cuisine
4 Sichuan cuisine
5 Zhejiang cuisine
6 Shandong cuisine
7 Jiangsu cuisine
8 Fujian cuisine

中国的菜系，是指在一定区域内，由于气候、地理、历史、物产及饮食风俗的不同，经过历史演变而形成的一整套自成体系的烹饪技艺和风味，并被全国各地所承认的地方菜肴。

3 Look at the dishes and learn their names. Discuss with your friend which dishes the children are describing.

Stinky tofu, Anhui
安徽臭豆腐

Oyster omelette, Fujian
福建蚝饼

Roast goose, Guangdong
广东烧鹅

Steamed fish head with chilli, Hunan
湖南剁椒鱼头

Yangzhou fried rice, Jiangsu
江苏扬州炒饭

Kung Pao chicken, Sichuan
四川宫保鸡丁

Longjing shrimps, Zhejiang
浙江龙井炒虾仁

Braised sea cucumber, Shandong
山东炖海参

I love spicy food! Which dishes are spicy?
Kung pao chicken, steamed fish head with chilli

It smells funny but tastes good!
Stinky tofu

Wow! Crispy skin and juicy meat!
Roast goose

Seafood is my favourite.
Oyster omelette, Longjing shrimps, braised sea cucumber

I'm a rice lover!
Yangzhou fried rice

习俗：北方常以牛羊肉做菜；南方喜食鱼、肉；沿海地区则多以海产品做菜。

气候：一般说来，北方寒冷，菜肴以浓厚、咸味为主；华东地区气候温和，菜肴则以甜味和咸味为主，西南地区多雨潮湿，菜肴多用麻辣浓味。

4 Did you know that the staple foods in southern China and northern China are different?

介绍完中国的两大类主食后，可问问学生他们的主食一般是什么。

Rice is a major staple food in southern China. Cooked rice, usually white rice, is the most commonly eaten type.

We eat rice every day.

Flour-based foods, such as noodles, Chinese dumplings and steamed buns, are the most popular staple foods in northern China.

5 Desserts are also popular in Chinese cuisine. They are served after meals. Look at a few examples.

Cold or hot	Cold	Hot

甜品是一个很广的概念，大致分为甜味点心和广东式的糖水。甜品在中国有悠久的历史，远在三千年前的商代，

人们就在隆冬季节把冰块储藏起来供夏日用。

6 Tea plays an important role in Chinese dining culture.
Have you tried Chinese tea before? 茶的主要味道来自茶叶，因此茶叶对茶的品质影响是最大的。除了茶叶外，水质也十分重要。

茶叶

Tips on Chinese dining 中餐小知识

Look at some tips on Chinese dining.

In traditional Chinese dining, dishes are shared between everyone. In restaurants, round tables with a turntable at the centre are often used for easy sharing. Tea is almost always provided.

Chopsticks are the main eating utensils in Chinese dining. They can be used to cut and pick up food.

Practise using chopsticks with me!

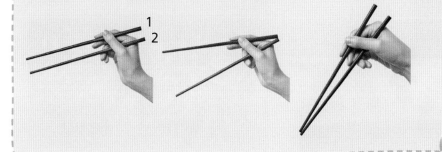

先用大姆指、食指和中指拿起图中高一点的筷子1，再在虎口放图中低一点的筷子2，同时用无名指抵住，对齐筷尖。夹食物时，张开、合起高一点的筷子，稳住低一点的筷子即可。

5 Tourist destinations 旅游目的地

Reasons for visiting China 来中国旅游的原因

Each year, tourists from around the world visit China. Do you know what they love about China? Look at the pictures and see what China has to offer.

Natural scenery
九寨沟
黄山

Architecture
布达拉宫
黄鹤楼

Culture
苏州文庙
舞狮

History
明孝陵神道
故宫博物院

Life style
太极
苗族舞蹈

Popular tourist destinations 热门旅游目的地

1 These ten places are among the most popular tourist destinations in China. Have you heard of them before?

北京	成都	广州	杭州	香港
Beijing	Chengdu	Guangzhou	Hangzhou	Hong Kong

丽江	澳门	上海	西安	阳朔
Lijiang	Macau	Shanghai	Xi'an	Yangshuo

2 Beijing, the capital city of China, is a place where old meets new. Look at some of the historic sites and modern tourist attractions. Which one do you like best?

the Forbidden City

故宫是中国明清两代的皇家宫殿，旧称为紫禁城，是世界上现存规模最大、保存最为完整的木质结构古建筑之一。

Beijing

the Summer Palace

颐和园是清朝的皇家行宫和大型皇家园林，巧妙结合了人工建筑与自然山水。颐和园为世界文化遗产。

Sanlitun

三里屯是北京时尚潮流生活地标。

the National Theatre

国家大剧院造型独特，一池湖水以及外围的绿化环境，体现了人与艺术及自然和谐共融的理念。

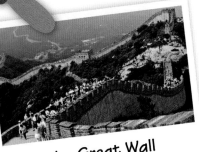

the Great Wall

长城又称万里长城，是中国古代的军事性工程，也是世界十大奇迹之一。

3 **Look at the popular tourist attractions in the other nine places. Help the children find the most suitable places to visit.**

卧龙是大熊猫主要栖息地之一。

Wolong National Nature Reserve, Chengdu

the Terracotta Army, Xi'a

兵马俑是中国秦朝皇帝秦始皇的陵墓。

Old Town of Lijiang, Lijiang

丽江古城是中国以整座古城申报世界文化遗产获得成功的两座古城之一。

the Li River, Yangshuo

漓江是中国重点风景名胜区，它的山、水、洞被称为三绝。

Canton Tower, Guangzhou

广州塔是一座电波塔，有广播电视发射、文化娱乐的功能。

提醒学生对应图片和地图上的地点，也可说说这些景点的特色，或上网搜寻相关资料。

陆家嘴摩天大楼天际线代表了中国近现代
经济发展的典范。

Lujiazui skyline, Shanghai

西湖是观赏性淡水湖泊，其文化景观于
2011年被列入世界遗产名录。

West Lake, Hangzhou

**the Avenue of Stars,
Hong Kong**

星光大道是一个以香港电影为
主题的景点。

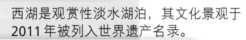

the Ruins of St Paul's, Macao

大山巴牌坊是澳门天主之母教堂
（圣保禄教堂）正面前壁的遗址。

参考答案：

I love animals.

成都

I like taking pictures of
beautiful sceneries.

阳朔
上海
杭州

I'm interested in
Chinese history.

西安
丽江
澳门

Arts 艺术

中国艺术主要是指具有五千年历史的中国传统文化艺术，如书法、国画、工笔画、音乐、戏曲、诗歌。另外还包括民间艺术、民俗文化、民族风情、民族信仰所延伸的宗教文化等等。

China's 5,000 years of history has given rise to its unique and various art forms. The following pictures show some of them. Look carefully. Complete the tasks and show your work to your friends.

Painting, calligraphy and literature

Painting

明朝松江秋

莫高窟壁画

徐悲鸿舞马

Literature

古代竹书

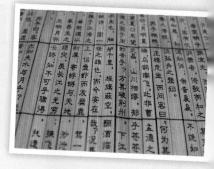

Calligraphy

王羲之书法

求道书法

Complete the Chinese painting.

Handicraft, sculpture and carving

鼓励学生上网搜寻更多的图片与全班分享，并说说自己对这些艺术品的观感。

Handicraft

剪纸

折纸

陶瓷

绳结

刺绣

风筝

Sculpture and carving

莫高石窟雕刻

石雕

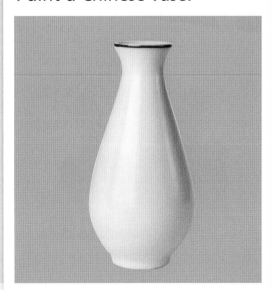

Paint a Chinese vase.

Performing art

中国的戏曲由文学、音乐、舞蹈、美术、武术、杂技以及表演艺术综合而成，约有两百六十多个种类，包括京剧、昆曲、粤剧等等。

京剧

昆曲

粤剧

皮影戏

杂技

木偶戏

Paint an opera mask.

告诉学生工艺美术性脸谱来源于舞台，学生可根据自己的想象绘画出色彩图案变化多样的制品。而在舞台上，演员是根据剧情和剧中人物的需要，用夸张的手法在脸上勾画出不同颜色，不同图案和纹样的脸谱。

民族舞

民族舞

民族乐器是代表着中华传统音乐文化的乐器。现在较为流行的有琴、筝、箫、笛、二胡、琵琶、丝竹、鼓等。

古筝、竹笛演奏

二胡、阮演奏

Architecture

紫禁城

苏州老民房

天坛

昆明八角亭

Draw a Chinese-style building.

中国古代建筑的类型很多，主要有宫殿、坛庙、寺观、佛塔、民居和园林建筑等。

OXFORD
UNIVERSITY PRESS

Oxford University Press is a department of the University of Oxford.
It furthers the University's objective of excellence in research, scholarship,
and education by publishing worldwide. Oxford is a registered trade mark of
Oxford University Press in the UK and in certain other countries

Published in Hong Kong by
Oxford University Press (China) Limited
39th Floor, One Kowloon, 1 Wang Yuen Street, Kowloon Bay,
Hong Kong

Photographs for reproduction permitted by Dreamstime.com

China National Publications Import & Export (Group) Corporation is an authorized distributor of
Oxford Elementary Chinese.

Please contact content@cnpiec.com.cn or 86-10-65856782

ISBN: 978-0-19-082365-8

10 9 8 7 6 5 4 3

Teacher's Edition
ISBN: 978-0-19-082368-9

10 9 8 7 6 5 4 3 2